HIDDEN WEDDINGS

HIDDEN WEDDINGS

SELECTED POEMS

Gerrit Achterberg

Translated by Michael O'Loughlin

RAVEN ARTS PRESS

Hidden Weddings
is first published in Dublin by
The Raven Arts Press
P.O. Box 1430
Finglas
Dublin 11
Ireland.

ISBN 1 85186 022 3 (softback)
    1 85186 023 1 (hardback)

Raven Arts Press receive financial assistance from The
Arts Council (An Chomhairle Ealáion), Dublin, Ireland.
These translations have also been funded by The Arts
Council Authors' Royality Scheme.

Raven Arts Press would also like to acknowledge the
financial support of The Netherlands embassy in the
production of this title.

Designed by Dermot Bolger and Susanne Linde. Cover
design by Susanne Linde. Typeset by the Carlow
Nationalist, Ireland.

4

CONTENTS

INTRODUCTION

Gerrit Achterberg, regarded by many as the major Dutch poet of this century, was born in Langbroek in 1905 and died in Leusden in 1962. On some levels, his life was uneventful. After short periods as a schoolteacher and civil servant, he devoted himself entirely to the writing of poetry, publishing many collections and accumulating honours and literary prizes. However, this quiet existence was marred by periods of erratic behaviour, the fruits of a mental illness. During one of these periods he shot a woman dead and was hospitalised for a number of years.

Achterberg's poems fill a volume almost a thousand pages long, and to a great extent they are a systematic exploration of a single theme. This is the great Orphic theme, the recovery of a dead beloved from the underworld, through the power of poetry, language at its most concentrated. For Achterberg, poetry was a matter of supreme seriousness, literally a matter of life and death. The engine which could power this Orphic task was a conceit, and Achterberg is in every sense, a metaphysical poet. The conceit is that the dead beloved is present in the world around him as a sort of gestalt — an age-old conceit, but Achterberg's originality lies in the lengths he went to to realize it. This conceit forms a bridge over the boundary between language and reality, between the timeless world of language and the world of life and death, which is situated simultaneously beyond the edges of the physical world and under the deepest layer of the human mind.

Achterberg called his collected volumes of poems 'Cryptogams' or 'hidden weddings', and it is at this boundary that the hidden wedding between life and death takes place, the visible evidence of which is the poem.

Central to this approach to poetry is a belief in the magical power of the word. This power is based on the idea that in the beginning was the Word, perhaps most clearly formulated by the kabbalists, who believed that all human life is present in the letters of the alphabet. Language forms an immense mirror, in which past, present and future, the living, the dead and the unborn, are all contained. Just as the mirror abolishes dimensional differences, so life and death are brought onto the same plane, and intercourse between them becomes possible. By building a mirror in language, a poem, Achterberg can translate, that is, move the dead beloved from one plane of existence to another, from the material world in which she is dead, into the world of language, where a kind of life is available to her.

The poem stops time. Achterberg does not see life and death as being of a different nature: they are separated by one dimension, time. But just as energy can be thought of in terms of mass and speed, that is, time, so Achterberg abolishes the difference between life and death by reducing it to an equation of energy: one which can be solved. Achterberg, in a sense, is the poet of relativity. If energy is thus interchangeable, he will attempt, in his poems to create force fields, systems of energy, which can be transferred to her, bestowing life. In the hermetically sealed poem, time is repealed:

STATUE

A body, blind with sleep
stands up in my embrace.
I feel how it labours.
Death's doll.
I'm an eternity too late.
And where is your heart's beat?

The dense night holds us together,
compacts us of each other.
"For God's sake don't let me go,
my legs have snapped",
you whisper against my breast.

It's as if I bore up the world.
And slowly comes the moss
creeping up over our statue.

The poem is a verbal machine, its energy residing in the tension and balance between its parts. It is language worked upon, and charged, racked up to the level of intensity which will always produce this spark; having the quality, as has once been said, of a piece of ice continually melting on a hot stove. In lines which seem to offer instruction to his translators, he wrote:

"Every series, any connection,
taken from whatever language, will suit
as long as they're at the proper tension."

The poem exists in the relationship between its parts, which are always interchangeable, if an equivalence is preserved.

This approach to poetry determines the formal expression of his work. He uses rhyme and strict metres to an extent rare in the works of poets in this century; not, however, to suggest or express an ordered and static view of civilisation, but to literally seal in the poem, close the energy system. In the Dutch language, the word 'dichten' means both to write poetry and to seal up holes, and Achterberg makes that pun central to his work in a manner reminiscent of Joyce. In his long poem 'The Ballad of the Gas fitter', the poet takes on the persona of a gas fitter, a man whose job is to seal up leaks. Puns anagrams, idiosyncratic spellings, are all important to him, as they were to the kabbalists, because they show how opposites can be reconciled and strange weddings revealed, how death can be repealed, not just in a whole oeuvre, or even in an individual poem, but in a word itself, like Joyce's 'wakes' and 'cropse'. Puns are important nodes of verbal energy, like the neologisms he often uses, and which the Dutch language is particularly rich. in. Energy is eternal, it simply changes form, and it is form 'which triumphs over the worm'. He ransacks the specialised vocabularies of science and technology, sources of potential energy, discerning the lineaments of the dead beloved in their internal relations and connectedness, in a manner which is sometimes the verbal equivalent of Salvador Dali's 'critical paranoia'. Few poets are more sensitive to the energies and valencies of individual words.

If Achterberg is very much a poet of his time, he is also a poet of his place, and language. The landscape of his poems is in ways, a very Dutch one: austere, tightly controlled, with infinite horizons, a victory over nature by diligence, imagination, and technical ingenuity. His range of symbols, is sometimes peculiarly Dutch. Even with languages as close to each other as those of Western Europe, the translation of certain nouns can cause difficulties. Normally, the habitual reader of translated poetry makes automatic compensations. If we come across the word 'heart' or 'soul' in translations of Spanish or German poetry, we automatically read them as being the particularly Spanish or German version of those entitles, reinforced by other readings, and our knowledge of those cultures. A word like 'house', on the other hand, which occurs often in Achterberg, has a particular resonance which is difficult to grasp for the non-Dutch reader. To a great extent, with Dutch, he is reading in the dark: or rather he sees a few brightly lit windows, like the art of the seventeenth century, but not the shadowy house around them. That is why, in my choice of poems, I have attempted to pick those which I hope illuminate each other to some small degree, and help to build up some of those resonances within the limits of a small volume of translations.

— Michael O'Loughlin.
Amsterdam,
Oct. 1987.

DREAM JUDGEMENT

The clock presides over the room,
monotonous laws
are murmuring in the evening,
no one can oppose its rules,
no one may pass.

Today I stand accused,
tonight I lie, awaiting judgement.
A hush in the chambers,
only the cupboard's breathing,
a mother who sees me.

Outside, wind and rain
implore and defend
outside, wind and rain
implore and encircle
the judge with their arguments.

Jingling dread
minutes, minutes;
hours gasp forward
and four walls plead
for a single word ·
of pardon before the morning,
for an answer of pardon,
for an answer before the morning

HULSHORST

Hulshorst, your name
is like abandoned iron,
your station rusts among
the firs and the bitter evergreens;
where the northbound train pulls in
with a god-forsaken screeching,
lets no one off, lets no one on,
o minutes in which I can hear
the gentle fluttering
like an ancient legend from your forests;
grim bands of brigands, rank and crude
out of the white backwoods heart.

THE NAMELESS . . .

By this bereft of purpose and name:
to go among men like a stone
lost among the stones of the street;
O dead number, alone in an empty sum.

Take me with your leaves, autumn,
this September is too white
to wander in alone
and I am like a lone leaf.
Let me be earth again
with earth above me;
the only mould which stayed me
is gone.

THIS POEM . . .

This poem deposes the one before it.
I'm again my own subordinate.

Until in the end it becomes clear
who's the vassal, or master, here.

Between my self and my life
there's still an undug grave.

But apart from all this
there's still the song to be sung
— there's still a song to be wrung

from death, her body's song,
the song of which her body is
the immaculate conception

and of which death isn't lord
within this word.

BULWARK

A spent secret subsides
in my limbs;
it could have been a child,
I think, or some such marvel;
but in you, it died.

Because of the darkness we share
the stars stand still
in me, are petrified;
the animals flee from me;
only the word persists
in greeting you with eternity
retained in bloom and time.

DEATH SONG

Song of death,
do not fall silent
before the universe wholly revealed
which won't let her be found
in street after empty street;
it is only round.

Think of it only as an image,
though desolate and blind
lest her state become unknowable
to this mind.

GRIEF

Grief, I deny
the sun its light,
the seeing their sight
and this universe its balance,
death the right
to any judgement
which detaches her from me.

Do not shun me, but
lay out eternity's mantle:

I lie in darkness, her double
except for a breath a moment.

WORD

You have entered and become the earth.
The rain has sunk down into you;
into you, the snow subsides.
The wind whips you naked.

The light is still in your eyes
as if you had woken this morning.
But they follow neither sun nor moon.
They touch no star.

As far as my blood is concerned
you are sated and replete
with every element.

And yet there must exist the word
which coincides with you.

'BEUMER & CO'

The skeletons in the cupboards
are exposed.
The floors are dying of shame.
The lamp looms large and low
because the table's been taken away.

They, who have come upstairs,
are wrecking blindly
what was once locked up; each object
is robbed of its destiny;
but love is of God
and God is love. Amen.

The inner door
is now the outer.
The glass dies
at the hand of the horde.

The mirror with eternal light
yields slowly, face down,
and closes the room.
Cobwebs cover it.

Where divan and darkness once stood,
their secret is out —
a woman's shoe was found.
But love is of God.
And the dogs will stand without.

MATERIAL

As if I'd never slept by your side
you've reverted to what you were
before you were created by God:
wind, earth, language
for a song as yet unborn;

in the presence of a universe
awaiting His next command;

because I am still breathing here.

DEBIT

I am the bitter residue,
on this side of God,
of our fate fulfilled in you.

To be able to find an ultimate
name for the beloved,
with which to dazzle the universe
before I myself become nameless.

It is my only debit.

The word was God in the beginning.

HOUSE

House, I dwell in you still.
Your lamps are glowing in my soul
as if it coincided with you,
and distance cannot intervene
to wedge its darknesses in between
the light of then and now.

In me, your things have the heavy radiance
of eternity, there is no difference
between this and death,
except that I still possess
the time, where it couches itself
in a verse.

DEAD FLOWERING

Out of our petrified
shared past, they break loose,
the posthumous lamentation
of our togetherness,
henceforth doomed
to be word and grave;

as for you:
out of the unyielding grip
the distressed roses
break open their white,
this is the fragile
afterdeath, opening now
in death's climate.

PASSWORD

Bent over her purgatory,
at the edge of this universe,
the soul parleys with nothingness;

to grant her the prospect
to which she's entitled
under love's protocol, before which
death calls his halt;

unless my song finds the password
which blinds him.

SPOTLIGHT

Face to face with the song's secret
death removes its veil;
metre after metre is exposed,
and from chorus to chorus revealed
in this sun's radiance: ash and loss
and my throat's hoarse echo,
everything that is concealed
to love, comes into view:
fixed in chalk-white residue,
your destiny, unfulfilled.

THAW

I have no other blood than this,
soaked in the light-skeins
of your immortality,
broken in a death notice.

Sometimes the flames blaze up again
as once before, and I lose track of time
in the double eternity
of body and poem.

But patches of darkness retreat
under the snow of your departure,
forming holes in the white:
rot, which slowly bites deeper.

AUTUMN

Eternities of mouth and womb
lie rotting in these lines.
The leaves fall on autumn's wharves.
Nothing is certain except the tomb.

TRANSPARENT

The night turns transparent as a September afternoon.
Dazzling, a female body is released.
I feel my desolation eased.
She takes me by the hand. I cry: I am degraded,
do not touch me. But weeping, she takes me in her embrace.
We break water, which shivers, shivers.
This is her realm, which remembers ours.

WORD AND DEATH

The words which I need
for this poem's existence
are embodied in your form,
are embedded in your hair,
are your eyes' radiance.

But all this, you said,
disintegrates when I slacken;
and as for me: it is only this conceit
which gives my song its balance.

FACE

Breasts ascend like stars
in the zenith of my lust for life.

In the night below, which growls,
there is no beast which doesn't buckle.

But a face on high says:
this body only turns to verse
when you lay it in the earth.

BLACKBIRD

The early blackbird gargles
goblets of bitter wine:
a dream, which lumps into pain
in the bird's throat
because there is no holding back the dawn;
because the huge integral darkness
can no longer be shut in.

INVERSE

Out of this verse there are no reversions
Because on the floor, a body reclines
In which no dream will have its origins.

Word, object of its own attentions
Behind a closed countenance.

Incest of sentence with sentence
The fruit murdered in its rudiments.

O strophes without consequence.

ORPHEUS

The stern borders of death
have been crossed without light.

I felt a feathery resistance
that sank in me like lead.

I bend back the inanimate
and my being goes deeper
into the distant haze, the pale horizon.

Obstruction and shuddering
shut behind me like hair.

The last elastic gesture
of the now abandoned circle of life.

TRUMPET

Out of the trumpet
your body is born
steel-perfect and white,
life incarnate.
I keep my eyes shut
tight: it is true,
the pure ivory
I die for
sounds in my ear;
you triumph
over decay
and I experience
you, vein by vein,
hand, skin, hair.

DREAM PERFORMANCE

You have chilled your kisses
and exalted them to a dream performance,
where sleep waits attentively
to see if life and death's exchanges
will ever be exhausted.

We lie together in the moonlight:
a white silence, without names;

beginning, which snags in the end.

SYLLABLES

The whispering woods
leak tidings of you:
a sea of syllables,
too brittle for a verse
spills through me.
Dread and shame are fused
into flight.

I return in dreams
and your smile
hangs among the leaves.

EMPTINESS

Emptiness, which stayed
when you passed on,
has floated off, has
drifted like a desolate moon
and broken against me.
I thought of something alive,
powder, a hang of hair.

VACUUM

I approach you now without intermediary
— because in the song each word
has its own sudden perspective
which surprises like a new death—
(o realm enticed closer
sucked in from this side)
every verse is a vacuum
so that breath is drawn
across the edge.

HUNT

The hounds in my head
are hunting the word,
deep in the gorge of sleep.
The dream constricts.
The hour lapses.
. . . .
I will never completely wake
out of this night,
no matter how the morning light
knocks on the deaf magnificence.

CREPE

A glow which danced
rose-red in her limbs
and coloured her words,
is glazed back into this black,
the dim crepe of death.

SMOKE

Smoke of your being,
event
in the disembodied,
where there's no one.
Own brittle
confession
in blue falsehood,
now that it's autumn.

CELLOPHANE

Aquarium of light.
Filtered pre-existence
against the windows.
Parkview.
Solidified opening
to you, from here.
Iron entrance, driveway.
Not to be entered.
No admission.
Airtight
mica with cellophane.

ALUMINIUM

Angel of aluminium,
riveted in my heart;
shrunk to metal
and a thin jubilation,
knit in you.
Fetish and mascot
on my journeys in death.

FELT

It is a night of skin.
Chamois sleepmate.
Felt, enshrouding everywhere.
Plush moon gliding
over suede limbs.
Your lips graze taffeta
in this velvet grave.

ENERGY

The fire, in which you now find
yourself, warms my feet, I consider
the fact of how unconsumed you are
even in your carbonisations,
how ceaseless this journey
begun through metabolism
— and your being will be smaller
than any known number
or greater than the sum of all,
your existence is indelible
in the fire of the world
which is the other side of breathing,
man abandons himself right up
to his limits, and becomes his own energy
without knowing for whom or what
he became nourishment and source
of life, but in this song you veer
right round, and etherialise into form
which triumphs over the worm.

STATUE

A body, blind with sleep
stands up in my embrace.
I feel how it labours.
Death's doll.
I'm an eternity too late.
And where is your heart's beat?

The dense night holds us together,
compacts us of each other.
"For God's sake don't let me go,
my legs have snapped",
you whisper against my breast.

It's as if I bore up the world.
And slowly comes the moss
creeping up over our statue.

OXYACETYLENE

Loaded by death
with your loss, the word.
Tongue of flame
against the void,
which bolts its sheets
of steel between us,
to keep us apart
for the sake of a song.

QUANTITY

You no longer lie so compact.
The trains travel round in you
without wounding you.
Death has insufficient stone.
The stone has insufficient death,
for yourself, you've become too great,
for yourself, you've become too many.
What you once possessed as singular,
I can count now one by one
light years all around me.

STONE SONG

Words turned wrong
way round, are en route
to you, but you haven't even
got ears to hear them.

Sentences turned inside out
because your mind is gone.
A song to bounce off you:
stone against stone.

CONVEX

Your life's rubber stretches wide
beyond the epidermis
which circumscribed your body once.
You're finished with inner and outer.
The edges of the universe
which are everywhere and nowhere
sheathe you now, o bride.

BEING

Your being is swollen
with nothingness, now you can reach
back before your origins, transcend
the limits of your thoughts.

Everywhere your essence spills
out of you, nowhere
are you checked by anything
through which you could exist.

I³

Stripped of inception and decay,
you must be present for me;
I coincide with your line:
we have two points in common:
birth and acquaintance.
At the third contact
celebrated in the body
I lie with you on the same plane.
The fourth time that I find you
is at my death, then we will
be cubed together, and nowhere
will the one
be an absence for the other.

0.i

You repeat yourself like a decimal
which can't reach the sum
it tends towards, you fall short
of every contact, because
death never goes perfectly
into nothingness.

POTENTIAL ENERGY

Everything joins you to me.
Every stone has your fall,
each cipher your number;
the statement your story;
tongue your language;
abundance your instance.
You accumulate yourself in me
making raindrops dead weight.
You are borne on every wing.

TELEFUNKEN

The radio angels sing
magnets awake in me
on death's wavelength;
an ebony flotilla
of like forces
that alternates current with you
across vast intervals.

Their diamond larynxes
launch thousands
of jewels in me,
on which your domain depends.
I feel enormous,
overwhelmed by space.
Your being flows
into mine, ultrashort.

FLOWERING

I flower within to flower with death,
weeding and cursing the other growth.
I nourish her with myself, someday there'll be
a flowery grave which flowers endlessly.

CODE

The lifeforce which you once possessed
now spreads itself over the alphabet.
I piece together the keywords from it
and open the heavy lock to your death.

"God" can be represented in verse
by the letters, g,o,d,
in this order, but not necessarily,
other formations will also serve.

Every series, any connection,
taken from whatever language, will suit
as long as they're at the proper tension.

The poet, while writing, balances his words
for the skirmish of life and death
until the door swings finally open.

THE GIRL AND THE DRUM

She had found a drum to beat.
Then she turned to metal, ever her teeth.
and her two hands began tingling
to thump the drum with drumsticks.

To stand on stage with the drum
bent backwards into the straps
which bound her to the pounding
of this rumbling organ's tautened skin.

Her eyes are closed because she feels
the rhythm prevail throughout her body,
an urge which unleashes itself in drum rolls.
Sacrifice and dominance trade places.
Girl and instrument mate like beasts.
The living girl and the dead drum.

DREAM FATE

You showed me the rooms again tonight;
completely the same. It was the first
of a thousand times I'd see them.
You were still Madame, and I, Monsieur.

We stood where we would later live.
No legend had yet been woven around us.
It was like that between us for a while
and then we got to christian names.

In this death-sleep I've been able to return
by affecting other addresses
and leaving before I wake.

Maybe now I'd be a commercial agent
or would have stayed with my father in the village
and later married an ordinary woman.

But now that I'm awake it doesn't matter
what faltered and hankered at the threshold
and fate did not grant me a single step.

RORSCHACH

Maybe I'll find traces of you still
in some corner of England, or close by home.
We don't know exactly where death's debris
can unite with existing material,

nor at which latitude the beloved
makes her presence felt. I must, above all,
stay free for the next journey
and blindly live by what is known.

Some day, strange mountains shall loom up
in front of me, with chains I can draw,
the paths which approach the highest peak,
the lie of the valley where you sojourn;
folded over beside appearances;
a Rorschach test which needs no interpretation.

ORIGINS

Staying with the family for once.
We sit together around the table.
The same phrases and gestures
Amounting always to the same old thing.

I've got to be careful or I'll put
down roots again, I'm in constant danger
of becoming the victim of the scale
which weighs up all against a fixed past.

I've had enough. It's turned too sour.
The world obtrudes between then and now.
I'm going to leave as breezily as possible.

So as not to arouse premature suspicions
I say "god bless!" in the dead dialect
and cycle hermetic through the dour suburb.

SCAR

Engelien Hartveld woods. First symptoms
of sexuality. Later, the scar.
After fifty years a satyr is playing,
undisturbed, the same games under the trees.

The girl went on growing, even in my dreams.
Heavy with love, light as under water.
Early this morning, from deep in time
the hangover I never got round to then.

Surely Lena is still alive somewhere,
not to be identified from those school afternoons,
when the species was wasting its time on us

and she too is asking herself
where the undersigned ever ended up
who tonight stilled her youth's desires.

SCENARIO

From distant beginnings with you,
still a dot to the naked eye
they arrive in the present
their heartbeats against my rib cage:
concretizations. I feel a cablegram
go through my biography
to this late hour which strains
out of kilter.

Like wildfire, a stab of exultant
terror blazes a trail.
Maybe through this inflammation
I can, despite distance and age
come to some understanding with you
behind the facts' back.

But maybe it's just a comic strip
introjection, a comic book;
a playful cartoon of memory
or mnemonically a tic,
for which there is no remedy.
The dream keeps its big mouth shut.

SEWER

In what sewer have I ended up.
Laid together in hideous suppuration,
together we form one alloy of sickness's
sediment and the ghosts of poisonings.

Refuse of previous lives, never removed,
which eats through the dammed underground water
causes a dull fermentation in the soul.
There is mud and rubbish in our dreams.

OWN SEA

In you, o song, it doesn't matter
what the world deprives me of:
freedom, name, friendship, destiny.

I am filled the more with you,
the lighter I am immersed
in the abundance of your glory and mercy.

And this sea is never a wave short.

MIMICRY

I let the evening die
till the room is dead too.
Your image, lifesize,
finds its former animation.
A fear that is big in me
because of the other's baseness,
settles like a pond.
If he assails me,
at his hands
I will only remain
as this unresisting water
in which there is nothing
but your face before my eyes.

EPITAPH

Let me outdie this
with words cooled by death;
they thought, if we kill him
we will strip him of his song.

One day you'll see, on the floor
of my grave, letters of dust:
the song which, rotting, I have become.
But that's no longer any of your business.

BATTLEFIELD

The twilight falls like earth.
A dog is roaming Holland.
A long-toothed dog.
A big black dog is passing
through each and every land.

We are lying all around.
United no more.
What bound us together
died between our teeth.
The twilight falls like earth.

TRUTH

Dead one, I have rotted right down
to the song which I still must write:
nothing eternal can survive
which is not carved into the bone.

I have acquired nothing more than
this cosmic truth; and the assurance,
from a number of Dutch gentlemen:
it's a long road which has no turning —

but you are gone.

GEOLOGY

Cold is between us
Like an ice age, o Man.
You are solid rock.
I am alluvion.

You are state and decree.
I change daily, to become
somewhere, sometime,
new, uncharted territory.

NOTES

Hulshorst. A small village in a nature reserve, famous for its sandy soil, thus its "white" heart.

Beumer & Co. The title refers to a removal firm mentioned in a Dutch provincial novel.

Origins. Achterberg came from a strict Presbyterian background.

Sewer. The posthumously published collection, Blauwzuur, contained a number of poems dealing directly and sometimes bitterly, with his experience of hospitalization.

Battlefield. In the original, this has echoes of two famous Dutch nursery rhymes.

ACKNOWLEDGEMENTS

Acknowledgement is made to Mrs. J. C. Achterberg-van Baak for permission to reproduce these translations.

Many people contributed to this project with suggestions, elucidations, encouragement and logistical support. I would like to thank Mrs. J. C. Achterberg-van Baak for her kind cooperation: Maurits Mok and Mrs. R. Mok-Timmermans; Scott Rollins and Joost de Wit; and, above all, Jinke Obbema, for her invaluable lexical assistance.

The making of these translations was supported by the Foundation for the Promotion of the Translation of Dutch Literary Works, to whom acknowledgement is gratefully made.

The translations of *Orpheus, Trumpet, Dream Performance, Syllables* and *Emptiness* were commissioned by the composer Margriet Ehlen for her song-cycle *Eurydice.*